Presiding Ladies the White House

Containing biographical appreciations together with a short history of the Executive mansion and a treatise on its etiquette and customs

Lila G. A. Woolfall

Alpha Editions

This edition published in 2024

ISBN 9789362096968

Design and Setting By

Alpha Editions
www.alphaedis.com

Email - info@alphaedis.com

As per information held with us this book is in Public Domain.
This book is a reproduction of an important historical work.
Alpha Editions uses the best technology to reproduce historical work
in the same manner it was first published to preserve its original nature.
Any marks or number seen are left intentionally to preserve.

Contents

INTRODUCTION .... - 1 -

Martha Washington .... - 4 -

Abigail Adams .... - 6 -

Martha Jefferson Randolph .... - 7 -

Dorothy Paine Madison .... - 8 -

Elizabeth Kortright Monroe .... - 10 -

Louisa Catherine Adams .... - 11 -

Rachel Donelson Jackson .... - 12 -

Angelica Van Buren .... - 13 -

Anna Symmes Harrison .... - 14 -

Letitia Christian Tyler .... - 15 -

Sarah Childress Polk .... - 16 -

Margaret Smith Taylor .... - 18 -

Abigail Fillmore .... - 19 -

Jane Appleton Pierce .... - 20 -

Harriet Lane .... - 22 -

Mary Todd Lincoln .... - 24 -

Eliza McCardle Johnson .... - 26 -

Julia Dent Grant .... - 28 -

Lucy Ware Webb Hayes ....- 30 -

Lucretia Randolph Garfield ....- 32 -

Mary Arthur McElroy ....- 34 -

Frances Folsom Cleveland ....- 36 -

Caroline Scott Harrison ....- 38 -

Ida Saxton McKinley ....- 40 -

Edith Kermit Carow Roosevelt ....- 42 -

THE WHITE HOUSE ....- 44 -

OFFICIAL ETIQUETTE ....- 50 -

INTRODUCTION

America stands to-day among the greatest and most progressive of the nations of the earth; and as the law of nations from earliest times has been the decline and fall of one, as another rises to prëeminence, it would seem that this great land of ours is fast soaring towards the highest pinnacle of national attainment.

If a nation is great, it is made so by the men who make and enforce its laws, who fill its positions of trust, who manipulate its finances, and who prove worthy citizens of the land of their birth or adoption.

And who are responsible for the men?

Are not the women, the wives and mothers of the nation, the bearers of this great burden of responsibility?

No nation has ever risen, or can rise above the level of its women, and in no other country is this truth more obviously demonstrated than in our own beloved and favored land.

Reasoning thus, we find that the American woman not only holds a high position of trust, but it is conceded by all who know her, that she fills it worthily, and is capable of meeting the varied demands upon her with rare tact and skill.

There are no women in the world to-day who are more truly the cynosure of all eyes, than are our own. They stand in the glare of public life in the highest circles of their own land, and are closely allied to royalty abroad, participating in, or presiding at, many of the functions of almost every foreign court, and everywhere the homage which is their due is freely accorded them.

There are two attributes of the American woman which are undeniably predominant in her nature, and these are *adaptability* and *individuality*.

They are displayed by the members of all ranks and classes, but probably the twenty-five women who form the coterie of "First Ladies of the Land" in our republican court at Washington, have had as great, if not greater, opportunities for exercising these qualities than any who have entered only into court life abroad.

"Noblesse oblige" is true in all stations of life, whether it be the nobility of honorable living or of high social birth, but in royal circles there is a code of etiquette which is enforced from generation to generation, just as royal sons and daughters are born to royal parents, and so its followers abide by its mandates as a matter of course. In a democratic country like America, no such rule obtains, for the children of a President of the United States, after their father's term expires, may relapse into social inconspicuousness and seldom appear before the public, instead of, as in royalty, inheriting their father's official greatness.

We have but one instance of the son of a President following in his father's footsteps, and only one where a grandson did likewise. The wife of a President may have been born in affluence and social prominence, or she may have passed her early years in the humblest environment, as was the case with a number of the women who have presided at the White House, but in every instance the duties of hostess have been faithfully and creditably discharged, while natural ease, grace and tact, combined with this wonderful power of adaptation, have rendered the hospitality of the White House unquestionably refined, and marked by the highest breeding.

Some of the women who have held this exalted position have been called to it while little more than young girls, and others have assumed its responsibilities and obligations late in life, yet all have upheld the dignity of the nation of whose social life they were, for the time being, the highest exponents.

Can this always be said of the life at foreign courts?

When we consider the laxity and licentiousness of some of the so-called nobility, and the freedom of royal personages in their accepted code of morals, we realize that the life at the White House at Washington, makes for all that is pure in social life, having had no breath of scandal attaching to it in all the years since its establishment, and having set an example of moral righteousness for all the homes in the country at whose head it stands.

The individuality of each hostess has left its imprint upon the history of her time from the pomp and ceremony of Martha Washington's régime, to the greater freedom from restraint of that of "Dolly Madison." We hear also of the extreme "simplicity" of Jefferson's administration and the social festivities which marked Mrs. Grant's residence at the White House. Mrs. Polk abolished dancing, while Mrs. Hayes banished wine, from their entertainments. Mrs. Fillmore founded the library, for of books there were none when she was installed as mistress of the White House; and Mrs. McElroy marked the administration of her brother, Chester A. Arthur, with the acme of refined hospitality.

The list might be prolonged, but instances enough have been cited to show that while the women who preside over the nation's home at

Washington, must conform to certain accepted rules of etiquette, there is left sufficient scope for each to display individual tastes and characteristics, without in any way lowering the tone of the social life of the Executive Mansion.

The author who has with marvelous industry and good taste, written these condensed biographies of our country's most eminent women, deserves the thanks of all; yet such short sketches as are embodied in this volume, can give but little knowledge of facts concerning lives with so much interest attaching to them that a history of each would offer absorbing entertainment to the lover of biography, but they can serve to enlighten every intelligent reader sufficiently to arouse a desire for more information relating to these women, famous in the story of their country's social and political events, and to awaken a feeling of pride that these queens of a republican court have no peers in any foreign realm.

Margaret E. Sangster

Martha Washington

FIRST PRESIDING LADY
1789-1797

Martha Dandridge, of Virginia, was married at nineteen years of age to Daniel Parke Custis. At an early age she was left a widow with two children, Martha and John Parke Custis. In 1759 she married George Washington, thus becoming the wife of the first President of the United States. Accomplished, wealthy and fascinating, fond of ceremony, yet hospitable, her entertainments at Mt. Vernon were world-famous. The White House was not erected until after Washington's death, hence she never presided there. New York being the Capital of the Country during Washington's administration her court was held in that city, refined taste and abundant wealth admitting of appropriate display. Her patriotism was equal to that of her husband and led her through many trying scenes and privations during the Revolution. She died in her seventy-first year, having gradually failed in health since her husband's death, nearly three years previous.

MARTHA WASHINGTON

Copyright 1903, by Bureau of National Literature & Art.

Abigail Adams

SECOND PRESIDING LADY
1797-1801

Abigail Smith, of Weymouth, Mass., became the wife of John Adams at twenty. Ill health during her early years retarded her education, but her strong mind overcame this difficulty. Her letters to her husband and her son prove her mental powers and strong character, and many of them have been published on account of their literary and historical value. During her husband's term the Capital was removed to Washington, and, though the White House was not yet completed, and the city was only a straggling town, the ceremony of Washington's time was resumed there during her short reign of only half a year. In private life she was her husband's constant companion, until, at the age of seventy-four, eight years prior to her husband's death, she died, leaving the record of a unique life. She was the mother, as well as the wife, of a President, John Quincy Adams being the eldest of her three sons, and in this respect she stands alone.

ABIGAIL ADAMS

Copyright 1903, by Bureau of National Literature & Art.

Martha Jefferson Randolph

THIRD PRESIDING LADY
1801-1809

    Martha Jefferson Randolph, the elder of the President's two daughters, presided at the White House whenever possible during her father's administrations, his wife having died nineteen years before his election. The White House, however, during his terms, was practically without a mistress, although at times Mrs. Madison also acted in that capacity. Mrs. Randolph was eminently fitted for such a sphere, but was able to assume its duties only twice. Having received the advantages of foreign education and travel, and the continual association with men of letters, she was a most brilliant woman, and had her tastes been less domestic she would have shone in society. She gave her father unremitting care when, after his retirement from public life, he settled at his estate Monticello, where two years after his death her husband also passed away. Monticello was then sold and the remaining eight years of her life were spent among her children.

MARTHA JEFFERSON RANDOLPH

Copyright 1903, by Bureau of National Literature & Art.

Dorothy Paine Madison

FOURTH PRESIDING LADY
1809-1817

Dorothy Paine, a Quaker, first married at nineteen, John Todd, a young lawyer of Philadelphia. One year after his death, when twenty-two, she married James Madison. Her kind heart, frank, cordial manners, and personal beauty made her very popular. When she presided at the White House her tact, ready recognition of every one, and her remembrance of events concerning them increased this feeling. Although her entertainments lacked the ceremony of past administrations, "Dolly" Madison was considered a charming hostess. While she was extremely charitable, she always dispensed her husband's wealth with prudence and judgment. The war of 1812 showed her true nobility in many ways, and it was she who saved the Stuart portrait of Washington when the British were about to pillage and burn the White House. The Government bought from her Madison's Record of the Debates in Congress from 1782-1787, for $30,000.

DOROTHY PAINE MADISON

Copyright 1903, by Bureau of National Literature & Art.

Elizabeth Kortright Monroe

FIFTH PRESIDING LADY
1817-1825

Elizabeth Kortright was the daughter of a retired captain in the British Army, who, after the peace of 1783, remained in New York. She married Mr. Monroe there during a session of Congress, but later the seat of government was removed to Philadelphia, where they resided until 1794, when Monroe was made Envoy Extraordinary and Minister Plenipotentiary to France. Her husband's several foreign positions of trust obliged them to live much abroad. She saved the life of Madame de Lafayette, who, upon the very day of Mrs. Monroe's call at the prison, was to have been beheaded; but the powerful support of the American Minister's wife caused her liberation. Mrs. Monroe was elegant, accomplished, dignified and charming, and her "drawing rooms" were more ceremonious than those of Mrs. Madison. She died suddenly, one year before her husband, who spent the remainder of his life with his daughter Mrs. Gouverneur in New York.

ELIZABETH KORTRIGHT MONROE

Copyright 1903, by Bureau of National Literature & Art.

Louisa Catherine Adams

SIXTH PRESIDING LADY
1825-1829

Louisa Catherine Johnson was born and educated in London. She met John Quincy Adams there, and they were married in 1797. His father, becoming President, transferred him to Berlin, where she accompanied him. During Jefferson's terms America was their home, after which Monroe appointed Mr. Adams Minister to Russia, where nearly six years were spent. In 1815 he was made Minister to England. When Napoleon was returning from Elba, Mrs. Adams, traveling from Russia to rejoin her husband at Paris, after several escapes entered the city just after Napoleon's arrival and the flight of the Bourbons. Having graced such high positions, she was eminently fitted to preside at the White House, but ill-health incapacitated her, although at the time Mr. Adams was Secretary of State they entertained most agreeably. When Lafayette last visited America he was entertained by Mr. and Mrs. Adams at the Executive Mansion.

LOUISA CATHERINE ADAMS

Copyright 1903, by Bureau of National Literature & Art.

Rachel Donelson Jackson

SEVENTH PRESIDING LADY

Rachel Donelson, wife of Andrew Jackson, died the December before the inauguration. Therefore the position of Presiding Lady was accorded to her niece, Emily Donelson, wife of Major Andrew J. Donelson, private secretary to the President. His adopted son's wife, Sarah Yorke Jackson, presided at the Hermitage then, and for many years. Mrs. Donelson was very young when called upon to fulfil her social duties; but innate refinement, ease, grace, dignity and various accomplishments rendered her capable of adding much to this period's noted brilliancy. All admired her, even when party spirit quenched unbiased judgment. In all points of etiquette she was arbiter, the President deferring everything to her opinion. Her four children were born in the White House. Early in 1836 she returned to Tennessee, as her health was failing, hoping for renewed strength; but consumption developed, and her death followed in December of the same year.

RACHEL DONELSON JACKSON

Copyright 1903, by Bureau of National Literature & Art.

Angelica Van Buren

EIGHTH PRESIDING LADY
1839-1841

Angelica Singleton was presented by her cousin, Mrs. Madison, to President Van Buren, in 1837, and in the following year married his son, Major Van Buren. On New Year's day, 1839, she assumed her place as hostess of the White House, as Hannah Hoes, the wife of Martin Van Buren had died in 1819, leaving him a widower when elected President. This was a great loss, for she would have filled well the exalted position occupied in later years by her eldest son's wife. The next spring Major Van Buren and his wife went abroad, where they received most flattering attentions, attributed to their high standing in America, and also to Mrs. Van Buren's exceeding charm of features, form and manner, and long ancestral descent. They were invited to dine at the Palace of St. Cloud, where they were entertained with a cordial lack of ceremony by Louis Philippe and his Queen. In later life she was a society leader in New York, her death occurring in 1878.

ANGELICA VAN BUREN

Copyright 1903, by Bureau of National Literature & Art.

Anna Symmes Harrison

NINTH PRESIDING LADY
1841

Anna Symmes was born near Morristown, N. J., and early in life was left motherless. Her father, disguised as a British officer, successfully carried her to her grandparents on Long Island, where she remained until the evacuation of New York. Trained in godliness, her whole life echoed her early teachings. When nearly twenty she married Captain Harrison, later General, and afterwards President. While he was Governor of the Indiana Territory she dispensed liberal hospitality, being greatly loved and admired, and here in her home in the old French Town of Vincennes many happy years were spent. Her husband being much away, she reared almost alone her ten children, afterwards seeing one infant, three grown daughters, four sons and ten grand-children die during thirty years at North Bend. The thought of removing to Washington was distasteful to her, but as the President died one month after his inauguration, this became unnecessary.

ANNA SYMMES HARRISON

Copyright 1903, by Bureau of National Literature & Art.

Letitia Christian Tyler

TENTH PRESIDING LADY
1841-1842

Letitia Christian, of Virginia, President Tyler's first wife, was extremely delicate, and lived scarcely two years after his inauguration. She was lovely and gentle, highly accomplished and beautiful, greatly beloved by her husband and family, but seldom seen in public, therefore during his administration the White House had several mistresses. The duties of hostess sometimes devolved upon his married daughter, but were generally assumed by his daughter-in-law, Mrs. Robert Tyler, to whom were relegated the duties of permanent hostess until, in 1844, the President married Miss Julia Gardiner. The ceremony took place at the Church of the Ascension in New York City, and was the first instance of the marriage of a President, which fact excited intense interest throughout the United States. Mrs. Julia Tyler, for the remaining eight months of the term, filled her position creditably and gracefully. She died in 1889, having long outlived her husband.

LETITIA CHRISTIAN TYLER

Copyright 1903, by Bureau of National Literature & Art.

Sarah Childress Polk

ELEVENTH PRESIDING LADY
1845-1849

Sarah Childress, of Tennessee, when nineteen years old married James Knox Polk, a member of the Legislature of that State. The next year he was elected to Congress, continuing fourteen sessions in Washington, and Mrs. Polk held a high social position there owing to her courteous manners, dignity and many accomplishments. When she returned to Washington as the wife of the President, having no children, she devoted herself exclusively to her duties in that position. At her weekly receptions the custom of serving refreshments to guests was abolished. As she was a strict Presbyterian, dancing also was forbidden; nevertheless, she was very popular. She was a handsome woman of the Spanish type, dressed with refined and elegant taste, and was noted as a conversationalist, beside realizing keenly the obligations of her station. She survived her husband over forty years, living at "Polk Place," Nashville, the home they had hoped to share in old age.

SARAH CHILDRESS POLK

Copyright 1903, by Bureau of National Literature & Art.

Margaret Smith Taylor

TWELFTH PRESIDING LADY
1849-1850

Margaret Smith, wife of General Zachary Taylor, was the daughter of a Maryland planter. Domestic in taste and devoted to her husband, she lived much in garrisons and afield, making a home anywhere. She was without social ambition, and therefore had no desire to preside at the White House, preferring her quiet home at Baton Rouge, where she and her youngest daughter, "Miss Betty," were widely known and liked, and where she permanently established an Episcopal church. When her husband was elected President, she relinquished the duties of hostess to Mrs. Bliss (Miss Betty), then but twenty-two years of age, whose grace of manner and youthful charms relieved the formality of Mrs. Polk's previous reign. Their residence at the White House was suddenly terminated by the President's death, sixteen months after his inauguration. Mrs. Taylor died two years later, at the home of her only son in Louisiana.

MARGARET SMITH TAYLOR

Copyright 1903, by Bureau of National Literature & Art.

Abigail Fillmore

THIRTEENTH PRESIDING LADY
1850-1853

Abigail Powers was born in Saratoga County, New York, and reared in poverty. In order to help her widowed mother she taught from very early youth, although still a student herself. Fine health, height, fair coloring, delicate features, kindly eyes and an expression of humor, made her attractive, if not classically beautiful. At twenty-eight she married Millard Fillmore. In his early professional struggles her varied talents were devoted to his interests. When he became President she graced her position with ease; if possible, never neglecting any functions, but owing to feeble health late in life she often gave place to her daughter, Mary Abigail, who, though young, was a charming and dignified hostess. Mrs. Fillmore established the White House Library, no books having been there on her advent. Three weeks after her husband's term expired she passed away quite suddenly, leaving the memory of a devoted wife and mother.

ABIGAIL FILLMORE

Copyright 1903, by Bureau of National Literature & Art.

Jane Appleton Pierce

FOURTEENTH PRESIDING LADY
1853-1857

Jane Means Appleton, daughter of the President of Bowdoin College, and later wife of Franklin Pierce, was delicate in her physical and nervous organizations from early childhood. She was rendered more so, however, at the time of her husband's inauguration, by the death of their only remaining child, a son of fourteen, in a railway accident. Nevertheless she did not give way to her personal grief, but dispensed cordial hospitality from the White House, presiding at every function requiring her presence, and thus sustained her popular husband, although her own preference would have been for a more retired life. Unselfishness and great mental ability distinguished her; as she was a deeply religious woman, she materially influenced the Sabbath observances of the White House circle while presiding there. In 1857, after her husband's term expired, they went abroad for two years, but her health was not restored, and she died six years before her husband.

JANE APPLETON PIERCE

Copyright 1903, by Bureau of National Literature & Art.

Harriet Lane

FIFTEENTH PRESIDING LADY
1857-1861

Harriet Lane was left an orphan at nine years of age, and was brought up by her uncle, James Buchanan, who took great pains with her education. When he became Minister to England in 1852, she accompanied him and was a marked favorite in court and diplomatic circles. She was a handsome blonde of twenty, dignified, graceful, clever and an engaging talker. On her uncle's return to America, and his subsequent election she became mistress of the White House and was renowned for her charm, good taste and diplomacy. She entertained the Prince of Wales, now King Edward VII, while in America in 1860, and in recognition of this was an especially invited guest at his Coronation Ceremony. Shortly after her return to America she developed symptoms of a serious illness, to which she succumbed in July, 1903. After her uncle passed away, her great sorrows were the deaths of her husband, Henry Elliot Johnston, and her two young sons.

HARRIET LANE

Copyright 1903, by Bureau of National Literature & Art.

Mary Todd Lincoln

SIXTEENTH PRESIDING LADY
1861-1865

Mary Todd, born in Lexington, Ky., had from girlhood a supreme desire to become mistress of the White House, which, however, did not seem probable when she married Abraham Lincoln in 1842, but later her ambition was realized. She was small, attractive in appearance, inclined to stoutness, self possessed in manner, and would have enjoyed her high position had not the troublous events of the Rebellion prevented all festivities and converted the White House into a public institution. The death of her second son preyed sorely upon her, but when in 1865 her husband was assassinated, the shock was too great, and that, added to the blow of her youngest boy's death soon after his father's, partly unsettled her reason. Although she traveled much abroad, she never recovered, mentally or physically. She died of paralysis in her sister's home at Springfield, Ill., in 1882, and was interred in the Lincoln Monument vault with her husband and children.

MARY TODD LINCOLN

Copyright 1903, by Bureau of National Literature & Art.

Eliza McCardle Johnson

SEVENTEENTH PRESIDING LADY
1865-1869

Eliza McCardle, of Tennessee, married in 1826 Andrew Johnson, a tailor, eighteen years old, whose early education she superintended perseveringly until his learning exceeded her own. Her character was simple, true and unostentatious, the duties of wife and mother being always conscientiously fulfilled. Her health being undermined by suffering during the Rebellion, she was a confirmed invalid when called to the White House, therefore Mrs. Patterson, her eldest daughter, became hostess. She presided with simple elegance, ease, grace and remarkable tact during her father's stormy administration. Their home life was delightful, and when they left Washington the whole family was much regretted socially and by all retainers, as their popularity was widespread. Mrs. Johnson's influence over her husband was always very marked, and throughout his life she was his greatest helper and adviser. She survived him only six months.

ELIZA McCARDLE JOHNSON

Copyright 1903, by Bureau of National Literature & Art.

Julia Dent Grant

EIGHTEENTH PRESIDING LADY
1869-1877

Julia Dent, in 1844, became engaged to Lieut. Grant. The Mexican war separated them, but they married in 1848. Years of failure and poverty followed, but her faith in his ability survived, and when his military prowess made him famous, she shared his triumphs. Later, as the President's wife, she was most hospitable, entertaining extensively in private as well as in public life, making Grant's administrations, socially, very notable. When his term expired, General and Mrs. Grant journeyed around the world and met with a continuous ovation. A special feature of it was the dinner given to Mrs. Grant by the wife of China's Viceroy, which was the first of its kind. During her husband's last illness she was his constant nurse, and was always an adored mother. Her remains, with those of her husband, share the famous mausoleum, built as a memorial to him, on Riverside Drive, New York City, the site of which she herself chose.

JULIA DENT GRANT

Copyright 1903, by Bureau of National Literature & Art.

Lucy Ware Webb Hayes

NINETEENTH PRESIDING LADY
1877-1881

Lucy Ware Webb was born in Ohio, and married Mr. Hayes in 1852, the union resulting most happily. During her husband's military career she often visited him in the field and endeared herself to the soldiers by her gracious sympathy. Frank, cordial, hospitable and beautiful, she freely expressed her pleasure at becoming mistress of the Executive Mansion, winning many friends by her sunny smile and sincere greeting. She was very popular, although she displeased a certain few among her guests by banishing wine from the White House table, thereby gaining strong support from the temperance advocates. A fine oil painting of her was added by these adherents to the collection at the Mansion, Frances Willard making the presentation. During her husband's administration their silver wedding was celebrated, the occasion arousing national interest. She did not long survive her husband, who died at their home in Fremont, Ohio, in 1893.

LUCY WARE WEBB HAYES

Copyright 1903, by Bureau of National Literature & Art.

Lucretia Randolph Garfield

TWENTIETH PRESIDING LADY
1881

Lucretia Rudolph, born in Hiram, Ohio, married James Abram Garfield in 1868, soon after he became President of Hiram College, where both studied. The marriage was ideal, his wife's intelligent sympathy and cooperative ability aiding greatly in his advancement to his high office. Through the terrible ordeal of his assassination, painful illness and death, Mrs. Garfield was vastly sustained by her power of self-control. Her short stay at the White House proved her tactful and cordial in dispensing public and private hospitality, gaining for her the nation's love and sympathy in her sorrow. President Garfield's was the first mother of a President to reside at the Executive Mansion, although others had seen their sons thus honored. A fund of over three hundred and fifty thousand dollars was partially raised for the Garfield family before the President's death, and the knowledge of this was a great comfort to him in his dying moments.

LUCRETIA RUDOLPH GARFIELD

Copyright 1903, by Bureau of National Literature & Art.

Mary Arthur McElroy

TWENTY-FIRST PRESIDING LADY
1881-1885

Mary Arthur McElroy presided at the White House when her brother, Chester Alan Arthur succeeded to the Executive office upon the death of President Garfield. In 1859 he had married Ellen Lewis Herndon, daughter of Commander William Lewis Herndon, who, by order of the Government, explored the Amazon River in 1857, but she died in January, 1880, less than one year previous to his election as Vice-President. Mrs. McElroy was specially adapted to fill such a position from her natural tact and previous social experience. Her residence at the White House was therefore marked by graceful and dignified hospitality and the task of entertainment was greatly lightened by the extreme geniality of the President. Like her brother, she was of fine and imposing appearance. After the death of Mr. Arthur his only daughter Ellen Herndon Arthur, lived in Albany with her aunt, Mrs. McElroy, the son, Chester A. Arthur Jr., residing chiefly abroad.

MARY ARTHUR MCELROY

Copyright 1903, by Bureau of National Literature & Art.

Frances Folsom Cleveland

TWENTY-SECOND PRESIDING LADY
1885-89—1893-97

Frances Folsom, ward of Grover Cleveland and daughter of his late law partner became his wife in 1886. She was the first President's wife to be married in the White House and to give birth to a child there, the second daughter being born during her father's second term. As President Cleveland was a bachelor when elected his sister, Rose Elizabeth Cleveland, presided at the White House. Beside being a literary woman she earnestly and creditably fulfilled all social demands. Mrs. Madison and Mrs. Cleveland were the youngest wives of Presidents. The latter quickly won all hearts by her ease, grace and charming manners, and upon her return in 1893, she received a hearty welcome. Since his retirement from office Ex-President Cleveland's home has been at Princeton, New Jersey, where Mrs. Cleveland and her young daughters sustain the popularity of earlier years gained by them in the Executive Mansion at Washington.

FRANCES FOLSOM CLEVELAND

Copyright 1903, by Bureau of National Literature & Art.

Caroline Scott Harrison

TWENTY-THIRD PRESIDING LADY
1889-1892

Caroline Lavinia Scott, daughter of Prof. Scott, President of Oxford Seminary, was born in Oxford, Ohio. She married Benjamin Harrison in 1853, before he attained his majority. Nearly forty years passed in congenial companionship, before death deprived him of a faithful and devoted wife. She was talented in music and painting and had decided literary taste. She was also an earnest church worker and truly charitable. Her social bearing in her high station was dignified, womanly and hospitable, and her death during her husband's term cast a heavy shadow over its closing months. They had two children, Russell and Mary. The latter, Mrs. McKee, made her home at the Executive Mansion, assisting her mother most graciously in her many and varied social duties. After Mrs. Harrison's death, she assumed entire charge as mistress of the White House, until the close of her father's administration in 1893.

CAROLINE SCOTT HARRISON

Copyright 1903, by Bureau of National Literature & Art.

Ida Saxton McKinley

TWENTY-FOURTH PRESIDING LADY
1897-1901

Ida Saxton, daughter of a prominent banker of Canton, Ohio, married Wm. McKinley in January, 1871. She was a devoted wife and inspiring companion in whose sound judgment her husband placed entire faith, while her personal attractions were also great. An enduring sorrow, caused by the deaths, in infancy, of the two children born to them, added to a chronic physical ailment, rendered her an invalid. Therefore, when appearing at public functions she received her guests seated. However, the death of the President's mother early in his term, and the grave situation resulting from the war with Spain, suppressed the festivities at the White House temporarily. Mrs. McKinley sustained a terrible shock in the assassination of her husband, early in September, 1901, from which she has never entirely rallied, although she shows great resignation, and a devotion to her husband's memory as great as that bestowed upon him in life.

IDA SAXTON MCKINLEY

Copyright 1903, by Bureau of National Literature & Art.

Edith Kermit Carow Roosevelt

TWENTY-FIFTH PRESIDING LADY
1901

Edith Kermit Carow, the playmate of her husband in childhood and "perfect comrade" since their marriage in 1886, has transformed the White House into an ideal American home. She is a model housekeeper, and in spite of the exactions of time and duties, tunes her household in perfect accord amid the unusual stir of young life there. She is splendidly equipped for her arduous task by her delightful charm of manner, tact, and an unusual ability to connect names, faces and incidents. She is endowed with rare good sense, to which, combined with many winning attributes and accomplishments, she owes her remarkable social success. She has a charming ally in her step-daughter, Miss Alice Lee Roosevelt, a typical "out-of-doors" American girl, who shares with Mrs. Roosevelt's five children a mother's full-hearted devotion, which was so severely tested and so heroically demonstrated during their father's perilous absence in Cuba.

EDITH KERMIT CAROW ROOSEVELT

COPYRIGHT 1902 BY FRANCES B JOHNSTON

THE WHITE HOUSE

The site for the erection of the White House, or the "President's Palace" as it was termed on some of the earlier maps, was selected by President Washington and General L'Enfant when they laid out the city of Washington in 1792. The corner stone was placed in that year.

The plans were procured by competition, which gave the award to James Hoban, a distinguished young architect from Dublin, afterward identified for many years with the architectural work of the capital city. By the architects of to-day his design is considered to surpass anything of a similar style since constructed in this country. The White House was so called after the home of Martha Washington in Virginia.

According to the original plan, the building was 160 feet long. The North and South porches, constructed from designs made by Latrobe in 1803, were added twenty-five years after the first occupancy of the house; and in Jefferson's time and under his direction, terraces were built extending 150 feet east and west of the mansion. The West Terrace, enclosed in glass and otherwise disguised, became in time the Conservatory so dear to the heart of the Washington sight-seer. The East Terrace was removed about the time of the Civil War, but, happily, both of these were restored and beautified during the general making-over of the house in 1902.

The White House, when President Adams came to take possession of it in 1800, was neither finished nor furnished, and its surroundings were rough and unattractive, little or no effort having been made to reclaim the adjacent country from its state of mud and ragged woodland. From time to time Congress made small appropriations for the adornment of the Executive Mansion, and this money was spent more or less wisely by the several administrations in their efforts to make the official residence comfortable. An appropriation of fifty thousand dollars was made to President Madison after the fire of 1814 for the purpose of refurnishing; but despite the expenditure of more than two million dollars upon the furnishing and decorating of the building during the first three-quarters of a century of its existence, it contained but few articles of value at the time of the remodelling under President Roosevelt.

It was originally intended that the public offices should be separate from the President's home, and previous to 1814 the Executive Departments occupied small detached buildings in the White House grounds. But of necessity the President's privacy was invaded by the business of his office, until finally, during the war, President Lincoln set aside the second story of the East Wing for official business purposes. This invasion limited the accommodations for comfortable living and introduced a degree of publicity into the family life of the Chief Executive that was far from agreeable. But these and many other discomforts were at last removed by the construction of the new office building and by the remodelling of the entire old building. There is now little business of an official nature conducted in the house proper, and the East Wing has been reclaimed for domestic purposes. With the exception of the outside walls, scarcely any part of the building has been left unchanged. The old flooring, long in a dangerous condition, has been replaced by new, supported upon steel beams. The latest improvements in heating, lighting, and plumbing have supplanted the old-fashioned arrangements tolerated by many administrations. In this process, it is to be regretted that many nooks and crannies of historic interest have been obliterated, but it is comforting to know that the alterations will preserve in good condition and for a much longer period the main structure and the chief beauties of the old house.

The East Room.—It is difficult to realize in viewing this magnificent apartment that it was at one time used by Mrs. John Adams as a drying-room for the family linen. The East Room was not finished until 1836, and a bare, bleak place it must have been in those early days. In former times state banquets were held here, but, in more recent years, it has been chiefly used for public receptions. During the administration of President Arthur this room was redecorated and refurnished, and afterward no changes of importance were made until 1902, when, with the rest of the building, it underwent almost complete transformation. The walls previous to this period were hung with historical portraits, among them the Gilbert Stuart portrait of Washington, saved from the fire of 1814 by Mrs. Madison; but these were removed, as were also the pillars and beams of the old room, to give place to the present beautiful scheme of decoration. The walls and ceilings are now of white; the spaces over the doors and windows contain low-relief panels, each illustrating one of the fables of Æsop. The ceiling is most elaborate, but of delicate design; from each of its three panels depend the splendid cut-glass chandeliers, which have taken the place of the former larger, but less artistic ones. Four beautiful mantels of colored marbles are features of the recent remodelling. The draperies are of rich yellow silk.

EAST ROOM

Copyright 1903, by Bureau of National Literature & Art.

The Blue Room.—It is in this famous apartment that the President receives his guests upon state occasions. The room is considered the handsomest in the house in point of decoration, and also in its beautiful proportions. The floor is a fine, highly polished parquetry, and the walls are covered with a heavy steel-blue silk with yellow embroideries at the ceiling and wainscot. In the pattern of this embroidery and in the decoration of the ceiling and the window hangings the star is used with graceful effect. Each of the three windows is surmounted by a golden eagle. A feature of the room is the fine marble mantel with its supports representing sheaves of arrows tipped with gold bronze. When receiving in the Blue Room, the presidential party stands in front of the windows, but formerly they occupied the north end of the room. A heavy rope of silk encloses a passageway for the procession of guests, who must pass from the Red Room into the presence of the host and thence into the Green Room. This change is one of the many that were brought about by the rearrangement of the entire premises. During the administration of John Adams, the Blue Room was used as a sort of vestibule, its convenient location making it available for this purpose.

BLUE ROOM

Copyright 1903, by Bureau of National Literature & Art.

The Red Room.—In early times this was the anteroom to the Library and the Cabinet Room. It adjoins the State Dining Room, and by recent changes has been turned into a smoking room, except when it is required for service on receiving days. It is then used as formerly, in conjunction with the series of state parlors. Its walls are covered with dark red velvet and hung with historical portraits. Its marble mantel is one of those which formerly adorned the State Dining Room, the other was placed in the Green Room.

The Green Room.—In old times the Green Room was the family dining room. The present Private Dining Room was then used for state dinners. Like the Blue Room, its walls are hung with velvet; here, however, the color is an exquisite silvery green. Some of the original paintings which, are reproduced in the White House Gallery of Portraits of the Presidents, also adorn the walls of this room.

State and Private Dining Rooms.—The State Dining Room was enlarged in 1902 by the addition of a corridor from which the private stairway led. This necessitated the removal of that portion of the stairs. The room now measures forty by fifty feet and will accommodate as many as one hundred guests at table. The walls are of panelled oak, and the window draperies of heavy green velvet. Flemish tapestries of the sixteenth century are a feature of the room, which is further decorated by a number of heads—trophies of the chase in American hunting-grounds—arranged around the beautifully carved cornice. The furniture is of red mahogany; it includes two tables, the larger, crescent in shape, and the smaller a rounded oblong.

An interesting feature of the furnishings of the State Dining Room is the complete service of china and cut glass, manufactured from special designs made exclusively for the White House and selected by Mrs. Roosevelt from a number submitted to her for approval. The design is simple but rich in effect and the china is of the purest texture, the whole having been very costly. The glass, which includes many pieces, is of the best American cut.

STATE DINING ROOM

Copyright 1903, by Bureau of National Literature & Art.

The Private Dining Room has been remodelled in a style essentially colonial, with an attractive color scheme of ivory white and red. The ceiling is domed and the window hangings are of red velvet. The furniture in this apartment harmonizes with the general plan of decoration, it also being distinctly colonial in design.

The Library.—The room, which is oval in shape, is situated on the second story of the Executive Mansion and was once used as the President's office, but is now converted into a private sitting room. It was during President Fillmore's administration that the Library was first organized, an appropriation being made for that purpose. The low bookcases line the walls which contain over seven thousand volumes, principally literature of an historical and classical character, and chiefly of Mrs. Fillmore's own selection. She greatly deplored the lack of books in the White House and urged the need of a more extensive Library. However, it did not progress, as it should have done, and is not catalogued.

THE LIBRARY

Copyright 1903, by Bureau of National Literature & Art.

The Executive Office.—From the time of President Lincoln's administration the business of the White House began to encroach seriously upon the living quarters. The discomfort and inconvenience resulting from this combination of public and private life under one roof— and that a roof of very limited dimensions—had long been realized. Plans to relieve the situation were occasionally brought forward, but nothing was accomplished until 1902, when the reconstruction of the entire establishment took place. It was then that the one-storied and basement building was erected at the end of the West Terrace for the accommodation of the Executive Offices. The architects have placed the structure most effectively in its relation to its surroundings. It contains a Reception Room, the President's suite of rooms, the offices of the President's Secretary and Assistant Secretary, telegraph and telephone rooms and several other offices. The building is comparatively small and will probably give place to a larger one in the course of time.

OFFICIAL ETIQUETTE

As the State social functions in America are not hedged about by the privileges and prerogatives to which rank, station and birth alone entitle the holder in monarchical courts, the ceremonies, observances and ritual are, in comparison, simple and meagre. No special lessons are required nor are rehearsals needed to carry off with proper dignity any of the observances of state courtesy. Nevertheless, while there is an absence of that ostentatious display that marks the ceremonies of the courts of Europe, official etiquette in America is prescribed by a rigid code established by the highest authorities, which none dare disregard.

It is only natural that state receptions should be governed by more arbitrary rules than those which direct purely social intercourse. It must be remembered that when an official reception is held, it is always an official duty that is being performed. The state forms and ceremonies which have obtained in America have varied from time to time according to the usages of the day and the taste of the national hostess. They have, at times, been further modified by periods of national calamity, war and the death of immediate relatives, but through all this variation and modification there has run the golden thread of democratic simplicity so dear to the national heart.

The period of Washington's administration must be regarded as a time of transition. Nor is it to be wondered at that much formality and stateliness marked the dispensation of national hospitality in the beginning of the nation's development. The term "colonial" is to-day associated in our minds with a courtly, stately conventionality peculiarly its own. Men and women of that time, who either at first hand or through their mothers and fathers, had received their education in courtesy, grace and proper behavior from the customs of England, could not easily shake off that second nature and no doubt fretted over the meagre means of gratifying their wishes; but as soon as they were cut off by their own desire from this influence and became self-dependent, that pure simplicity nurtured by individual worth became evident. It is not surprising that in the earliest period the Executive Mansion was a place of stately and continuous reception and that Martha Washington is famous for the dignity, grace and splendor of her social reign: but, on the other hand, the simplicity of Jefferson's time has passed into a proverb, and was such as to excite comment even abroad. The youth, gaiety and impetuous brilliancy of "Dolly Madison" contributed largely to the breaking down of much of the severity and conventionality which preceded her time.

The President is the leader of social as well as of official life. While he is accessible to all to the extent that all may call upon him, he is not expected to return any visits. He, of course, has the privilege of calling upon a friend. The same is equally true of the wife of the President. He is always addressed as "Mr. President." He can not leave the country, and in this respect is under greater restrictions than are any of the crowned heads of Europe. Under this "unwritten law" a foreign legation in Washington is construed as being foreign ground and may not be entered by the President. Neither can he set foot upon a foreign vessel. The only formal calls that he can make are those upon a President elect, an ex-President, a President or reigning monarch of a foreign state visiting Washington. It is regarded as an impropriety for him to accept an invitation to dinner at any time or to receive other than very intimate friends on Sunday. He carries no personal card but one reading simply "The President." He can not accept valuable gifts and if such are tendered they are usually placed in the National Museum. It is not expected that he should allow himself to be interviewed.

The Chief Justice of the Supreme Court ranks next to the President socially. He takes precedence over all others because his office is for life while that of others is only temporary. Below him in turn socially come the Vice-President, the Speaker of the House, the General of the Army and the Admiral of the Navy. It is considered one of the first duties of the Members of the House of Representatives to call upon these when coming to Washington. The social rank of women is decided by that of the husband or father.

The Inaugural Ball is the first social event in the life of the newly inaugurated President. It is always held upon the evening of the day of his inauguration, and partakes more of the nature of a reception than a ball for it is so largely attended that dancing is an impossibility. It is usually held in one of the departmental buildings. For several days after his inauguration, public informal receptions follow and a week or more is consumed in receptions during the day and dinners at night. These latter are classified, to a certain extent, so that all branches of the official service are formally recognized. Saturday is the official reception day at the White House. The public receptions which are held from the first of January until the beginning of Lent were inaugurated by President Jackson. The guests assemble in the East Room and as quickly as this is filled the President greets them as they pass out. The formal receptions are not held so frequently as previously, on account of the great increase in the number of Senators and Representatives. This is compensated for by inviting some Members of Congress to state dinners and entertaining others with less ceremony.

The scene at a formal or official reception is a brilliant one. The Government officials, the officers of the Army and Navy, and the foreign legations mingle together in uniform, and the ladies are not in full dress but in reception toilettes. Diplomats and attachés wear their court costumes. The President stands at the head of the line, next to him his wife who invites several prominent ladies to assist her in receiving. As the guests enter they pass down the receiving line until they have greeted all of the ladies of the receiving party. The daughters of the household of a state official are not invited to state dinners unless the daughter is the female representative of the family.

The general conduct of, and the social observances at these several ceremonies are the same as those which direct social observances elsewhere in good society. The cards of invitation and responses to the ordinary receptions do not differ from those in other American homes; but at the state dinners and official receptions, which are to be regarded in some sense as an interchange of international courtesy, the rules of attendance are very strict and no one would think of neglecting to attend without an eminently satisfactory excuse.

Milton Keynes UK
Ingram Content Group UK Ltd.
UKHW050242220624
444555UK00005BA/489

9 789362 096968